The Crushing Process
A Divine Call of God

By

Lora Johnson-Posey

Bloomington, IN Milton Keynes, UK

authorHOUSE

AuthorHouse™
1663 Liberty Drive, Suite 200
Bloomington, IN 47403
www.authorhouse.com
Phone: 1-800-839-8640

AuthorHouse™ UK Ltd.
500 Avebury Boulevard
Central Milton Keynes, MK9 2BE
www.authorhouse.co.uk
Phone: 08001974150

First published by AuthorHouse 4/12/2006

ISBN: 1-4259-2856-0 (sc)

Library of Congress Control Number: 2006902869

Printed in the United States of America
Bloomington, Indiana

This book is printed on acid-free paper.

In loving Memory of my precious daughter and angel

Saundra Deloris Johnson, born February 20, 1982, who went on to

be with Lord on her birthday. We will see you one day my precious

child in Jesus' Name

•DEDICATION•

I would like to dedicate this book to my family and friends but most of all to the hurting, displaced, misrepresented and shy individuals who feel that no one cares for them or sees their pain. I thought the same thing at one time or another in my life only to find out that God loved me above measures. He loves you when you do not love yourself or feel that you are worthless in the eyesight of man. It is not about man my friend; it is all about God and He loves you for whatever state of mind you maybe in at this moment. Trust Him with your life and He will change your way of thinking, your way of doing things and your way of life for His glory.

I thank God for my husband and my children for putting up with my shortcomings and with me. I delicate this book to my husband even more so because if it had not being for God using him in certain parts of my life, I would not be able to write this book and share with you all the things that I have gone through for the sake of God's love and the love of my soul mate. My high school sweetheart was a jewel in my life all those years we were apart and he is now a precious stone of gold from God. We were married on sweetheart's day, February 14, in 2002, and I love you dearly my love and may God continue to use you to keep me moving in the right direction with Him.

I love you all so much that words cannot describe it. To my husband Orlando Guy Posey and my sons Orlando Santrel Johnson, Kelvin Sanchez Johnson, Leander Rychard Posey, Jonathan Antron Magee, Orlando Takeem Posey, Justin Rachard Magee, and Jamol Guy Posey. As God continues to move through our family, I pray that you all become all that God has ordained you to be. A family that prays together stays together and we have giving God totally control over our household and whatever He has promised to the family, He has already preformed it before the foundation of the world, therefore, we will rejoice in it and be glad Amen.

Table of Contents

•FOREWARD•

In an age of anxiety, anguish, confusion and conflict especially within the community of faith...when so many are telling us to hold on, it is refreshing to attest to the witness and testimony of one who has been tried in the fire of traditionalism and survived by the grace of God and through the faith of God. This is the tread that ties the life of Lora Posey, my beloved daughter in the gospel and preaching ministry, together and holds her and so many other women like her.

God is looking for women who are willing to sacrifice their own personal agenda as well as popular public opinion for the kingdom's sake. Women have played such a major role in the life of the church but so often are overlooked as pioneers of faith.

I thank God for blessing Rev. Posey with the boldness to share with us her experience and walk of faith and growth for I already believe God for the deliverance of the many hurting, suffering and struggling souls that read these pages.

As you read these pages remember 2 Corinthians 10:3-5, "For though we walk in the flesh, we do not war after the flesh, for the weapons of warfare are not carnal but mighty through God to the pulling down of strongholds, casting down imaginations and every high thing that exalteth itself against the knowledge of God and bring into captivity every thought to the obedience of Christ."

Arthur L. Siggers
Pastor of Mt. Olive Baptist Church
Hattiesburg, Ms

•INTRODUCTION•

When God first started to deal with me in writing this book, I was not sure if it was truly Him talking to me. Most people have a hard time writing down their thoughts and their pains for others to read, just as I did. We do not want to expose the hidden secrets in our lives; but when we say to God that I want to be used by You then we bow down to His (God) Will and do as He has commanded us to do. I would have never guessed in my right mind that I would be preaching the Word of God, prophesying to the people of God, nor writing this book. Therefore, it goes to show us that we can do all things through Christ that strengthens us Amen.

Never in my wildness dreams would I have thought that

God would choose me to be one of His Prophetess who had issues with just being called to preach. In this book, you will find how my struggles lead to a divine call of God on my life and how He mainstreamed every avenue to get me to the place He wanted me to be. When we are lead my God, He leads us into the wealth places that He has for us. As I was seeking the Lord in my walk with Him, my mind stayed focused on Matthew 6:33 that said, "But seek ye first the kingdom of God, and his righteousness; and all these things shall be added unto you. What does this scripture really mean? What does it really mean to me? How did this scripture fit into my life as a child of God? How does this scripture fit into your life as a child of God as well?

I was not able to understand the meaning of this scripture until God taught me how to walk in this scripture through the Holy Spirit. Maybe you are asking how do you know that you are walking in this scripture. Well, one way to know is to break the scripture down in its elements or parts and define each one. First, God asks us to seek. What is He asking us to seek? He is asking us to seek Him first. How do we seek Him first? Seek His kingdom and all His righteousness. Not our righteousness, but His. We ask Him to come into our lives and save us. Then Matthew 6 tells us that we are to line up with His will for our lives. We are being transformed by the renewing of our minds to fit His image and likeness. Therefore, we are no longer our own but we are His. We have to be willing to give up ourselves for Him (God). God has a purpose for your life and my life. In order for us to achieve that purpose, we must allow Him to be in complete control of all that we do on this side and when we get to Heaven we will not have to wait to experience true happiness because we have experienced it on this side as well. The joy of getting to Heaven will be that we will not have to deal with Satan and his vices anymore. Everyday will be a glorious day Amen.

•CHAPTER ONE•

Life as a Child

I was born at the Charity Hospital in Laurel, MS to Mr. and Mrs. Leo Johnson on December 19, 1960. Both of my parents were married to other people once before they were married to each other; and what was so ironic about their union was that they were dating each other once before they married the other people in their lives. My Dad had a daughter by his first wife and my mother had three children by her first husband, a girl and two boys; my parents had four boys and me. I was the second child born with three boys under me. The baby of all of us died when he was eight months old. He fell somehow and hit his head; I was too young to remember what actually happened, but I do remember that it was one of the most trying times for my mother. I can also remember my brothers

1

and me would play together as if we were friends instead of siblings. We had our share of fights and so forth but we always enjoyed playing with each other.

My cousins and I along with my brothers enjoyed playing together as well. It was as though there were no other people on earth. I was like five or six at the time so there isn't too much I can remember from my young, young age. However, I do remember a lot at age eight. I remember age eight because it was during the time my sister by my dad's first wife came to live with us. We had never met her before and as children back then, we never thought of worrying about grown folks business like most children today. All we knew were that she was our sister and that her mother was not our mother and we just accepted that fact and moved on.

I enjoyed having a second big sister so much so that I spent a lot of time with her. Everywhere she went I would follow behind her. Even when she started dating, her boyfriend became my boyfriend as well. They would go places and I would go right with them as if I had being asked out on this date. In others words, I took over my sister's date. I can also remember at age eight sitting in Church with them one Sunday morning watching how the older folk would praise God and I lean over to my big sister and said to her, "I want to praise God like that some day. I began to really look forward to going to Church every Sunday because there were a stirring in my spirit. Finally at the age of twelve, I went to the alter to accept Christ as my Savior. I did not know the first thing about being saved, and was never taught how to maintain my walk with the Lord, so every time I would mess up I would go back to the Alter and get saved all over again until finally I just stop trying to be saved.

During the week everyday before we went to school, we had to do chores. Our bedrooms had to be clean and beds made before we left the house. We would always get up at five O'clock in the morning before the bus would run at seven O'clock to ensure that we had time to clean and eat a good hot breakfast. Five O'clock was the time we had to get up every Saturday morning any way regardless; so we were defiantly use to the rules of the house. We always had something to do before and after school. When School was out for the summer, we would hit the floor at five O'clock getting prepared to go to the fields.

My Dad was a farmer and he planted everything he could think of to plant. He planted peas, beans, greens, potatoes, corn, squash, you name it, and he planted it. We even had cotton at one time. He raised pigs, chickens, cows, cats, dogs, and horses to ply the fields. He still has cows, dogs, and cats 'til this day. Fishing and hunting was what he loved to do in his middle age days; now he only does the fishing because of his sleeping disorder that he ended up with from his years of being in the army. We had plenty of vegetables and meats to eat because my Dad would take cows and pigs to the slather house. Therefore, every free minute we had was with our hands at work around the house. We learn to work for what we wanted. We did not get everything we wanted except for sometimes at Christmas; we got those things that we needed the most. Nevertheless, most of all, my family and I got alone really well with the exception of my Dad being at the house but not in the house. His body would be there but his mind would be on his job.

My Dad was a workaholic; he thought that that was all to life. He thought that as long as he was bringing the money in the house and we had food on the table that that was enough, which was a good thing, but it was not everything especially to a child growing up. There were times in my life that I resented him for not spending time with me. Dad cared about coming home, eating a good home cook meal and resting up for the next job. I never really learn how to hold a conversation with the opposite sex because Dad never took the time to sit down and talk to us other than telling us what to do. I understand now that my dad was doing what he thought was the right thing to do because he says now that he which that he could do things all over again. I love my Dad dearly, but I could never get close to him. I did not know how to form a relationship with him the way my siblings and I had with our mother.

•CHAPTER TWO•

Life as a Teenager

When I turned sixteen, I was rebellious and hated the things that my Dad was doing. Every thing to him was work, work, and more work. My mom taught the girls how to be women and how to clean and cook but she also taught us how to spent time with one another. One day I was to stay home from the fields to tend to the house; my Dad did not tell me that I was to cook dinner while they were out. We were told numerous of times never to turn on the stove when there were not an adult in the house, so I did as I was told. When Dad got home from the fields that particle day, he went into the kitchen to get something to eat and I had not cooked. He got so angry with me that he slapped the living daylights out of me. Every thing that I had felt toward him came to the surface and

I talked back to him in such a harsh way. For a moment, I forgot that I was his daughter; that he was the parent and I was the child. I told him that I was not his wife, that it was not my place to make sure that he had a meal on the table, and when my Dad got finished beating my backside, I never talked to him like that again. There were times when I thought it, but it never left my mind, nor parted my lips again. My Dad really did not know that I truly resented him even the more after that because I never told him while growing up. I carried that resentment within me for years.

Growing up, I spent a lot of time with my mother and I think that was because I was a shy little girl and very insecure of who I was as a person. Most people thought that we had money simply because my dad farmed; most girls my age did not like me because they thought that I was stuck up, but in reality, I was afraid to be a person or bond with other people. When some of the girls really got to know me, they found out that I was just a scared, shy little girl. I don't mean to indicate or make it sound like that I did not associate with other girls or that I did not have friends because I did, but some of them my age were against me because of the little boys that admired me. I was not thinking about boys at that age because I was having issues in my relationship with my Dad. I pretty much hated boys, especially if they talked about my body. I was not what you call a typical teenager, I was very mature for my age and I can see those same qualities in my fifteen-year-old son now in the year 2005. My parents advised me that when boys talked under girls' clothes they did not mean them any good, so I believed what my parents taught me. My best friend was the same way I was, she would fight the boys if they would say things inappropriately to her. The little teenage boys had their eyes on me back in 1976, but my mind was on finishing High School.

There were times I would think about what if I got pregnant if I would fool with a boy, so I stayed focused on finishing school. My parents would always say, "Get your education before anything else" and that was what my mind was set on doing. It is bad that I did not carry that concept over into my college life as well and maybe if I had who knows where I could have being in my life today.

My Dad finally decided to stop farmer since all the boys had jobs and he could not maintain the planting by himself. So on weekends we got a chance to play sports with our Church team. During that time is when Doc really started to notice me. I was not sure if he was noticing me, or one of my teammates, which happened to be a great friend of my 'til this day, and I never tried to find out if he was or not because I ended up seeing him months later in 1976.

Doc and I went to the same Church, grew up in the same community, saw each other all the time and one day he started talking to me and our relationship, which started out being just a friendship sort of thing, blossomed into a beautiful love affair. The more he talked to me the more I started thinking about him in a special way. I did not know how to whole a conversation with him and whenever he would ask me questions, I would answer his questions and left it at that. Somehow, Doc became my High School sweetheart. My dad did not care too much for Doc because he saw him with all the other girls and it would really upset him because Doc would hang around in my face as well. Therefore, my Dad developed a dislike for him. My family did not own a telephone in the home, but I would always call him at a certain time of the day from my grandmother's house. We would plan sometimes on when to call and during those times, I found out that I was comfortable talking with him on the phone but could not talk to him face to face. I noticed that there was something wrong with the fact that I could talk to him over the phone but would clam up when I was face to face with him. That is when I knew that I was missing a stage of bonding with my dad. I understood the difference between bonding and communication of a dad and that of the opposite sex. My thing was that I was eleventh grade and I should have being able to talk to a boy face to face at that time and not have being controlled by my fears.

I finished High School in 1978 and started Jones Jr. College during the fall semester. Doc spent a lot of time at Jones in behind me while he was attending USM. We would leave campus some days just to be together which I found to be ironic because even though I could not talk to him face to face, I was not afraid to spend time with him. During one of those times, I ended up pregnant, which was the very thing I was afraid of while in High School; I did not know right away that I was pregnant but I had my baby in December of 1979 so I had to get pregnant around March of 1979. Once I found out that I was pregnant, I began to look back at the month of March and realized that a lot was happening with me in that month. The last few days of March, my older brother who was one of the boys by my mother first husband came into my bedroom while I was asleep and woke me up from an afternoon nap to tell me about a check that he wanted me to give to my mother. I remember fussing at him for waking me up not knowing that that would be the last time I would ever see him alive. He left the house that evening and was killed that night by a hit and run incident. I really felt bad for the way I had screamed at him that day. I struggled with my peace of mind after that and it was at that time that I found out that I was pregnant with my first child. So I justified my reaction toward my brother that day to my being pregnant but it still did not make me feel better about what I had did. We buried my brother a week later in April.

     I was six months pregnant before I finally told my family that I was having a baby. My Dad was hurt by my news but he stood by me and I think that was the turning point of my trying to work through my resentment of him. He showed me the love and support that I needed to survive the situation that I was in, but I still did not know how to love him. When my child was born, Doc denied him because he was in a relationship with someone else and I ended up having to deal with that problem as well as with all the other stuff that was going on. Whenever he would come around the baby or me, he would do so just to see if the baby was really his. Doc was one of the silliest young men in our community. He was young, dumb to life experiences, and had no respect for others feelings even though he came from a well-educated family; he was always taught the same things I had being taught about getting an education; he did not stop at High school. Maybe if he had being a girl (just a cop out, but worth mentioning anyway), who knows where he would have gotten in life. He was sowing his wild oats freely. I was just as silly as he was even though I had always being exposed to godly wisdom because I would sit in the present of older people, but did not know how to apply that wisdom. It makes a different when you know how to use what God has bless you with through other people.

All the time I was going through all of this stuff in my life, I knew that God was with me. In May of 1981, I ended up pregnant again by Doc and this time I hated myself for allowing this man to do this to me again and mind you, he was still in this other relationship. Oh! How I hated myself for that, how in the world could I have let myself get caught up in this mess again? I beat myself up so bad that I took it out on my unborn child. I wanted to kill my child. I thought of ways that I could do it, but the more this child grew inside of me I learn to love her more and more. August of 1981, Doc came to my house and inquired about my pregnancy and I look him straight in the eyes and lied to him that my baby was not his. I told him that it was someone else's child because I was sick of his games and I had allowed him to mess up my life again, and he was with someone else. All I wanted him to do was to get out of my life and I told him so. I was still in college after my first child was born and every summer I would work at the poultry plant in Collins while school was out.

I was still attending Jones Jr. College during my pregnancy

with my second child as well. Six months later, I received news that Doc was marring the other girl. I had our baby on February 20 of 1982. I was taking to the Charity Hospital, which was the same hospital that I had our first child and where I was born as well; but this time something was different about being there. The hospital staff that was on duty that morning around two O'clock was prepping me for delivery and as time drew closer and closer with the label pains, I began to brake out in a cold sweat and my pains were getting unbearable to handle, so I call for a nurse. They came in to check the movement of the baby and replied, "She still has not dilated enough to take her to the delivery room yet". I then said to the nurses that I could not have this baby, that something is wrong. One of the nurses answered me saying, "Oh! Yeah, you're going to have this baby; you got down there and got it didn't you?" Finally, a few hours later, the doctor came in and said how long has she being in label? The nurse's answered him and the next thing I heard him say was we need to get her into deliver immediately because something is wrong.

Once they got me into the delivery room they began to give me the Ethel gas, but I could still hear what they were saying. I heard the doctor say, "We are going to loose one of them". They worked and worked on me and finally the baby came, but I never heard her cry. I never heard a peek out of my baby, it was so quiet in that room and the atmosphere was so dreary feeling to me. They took my baby out of the room and did not bring her back and finally I asked them where my baby was? However, the Nurses could not tell me anything until the doctor came back, so they just tried to keep me comfortable.

When the doctor came back into the room, he told me that my baby had died. He said that she weight 10 lbs and some few oz., and plus she was born with a water head. I broke down and cried; I still cry 'til this day when I think about it or talk about it. When my Dad came to see me at the hospital, I asked him if he would make arrangements for my child to be buried before I came home from the hospital because after all the things that had being happening with me and my family since my pregnancy, I was not able to handle the burial of my daughter. My Dad did as I had asked, but there was one thing that my entire family did not know, probably still does not know today or maybe I told them and they do not remember that I was almost paralyzed after having my baby. I did not tell the doctor or anyone at the hospital because all I wanted to do was to get out of there and go home.

The first time I really notice that something had happened

to my right leg during my ordeal in the delivery room was when I was lying in my bed in the recovery room; I went to get out of the bed to walk around the hospital to rush my recovery process. I was going down the hallway after a few days of being in the hospital and collapsed on the floor. I managed to get myself up off the floor before any of the staff would find me and I made my way back to my bed. I would work my right leg whenever no one would be around to see me because I did not want the hospital staff to question me about why I was doing what I was doing. I would get up out of my bed whenever I could, trying to stand on it to strength it while all the time praying to God that He would help me through this. However, I never told anyone as long as I was lying there in that hospital.

My Dad buried my baby on a Sunday morning before he came to get me from the hospital later that evening. When I got home from the hospital, I had to deal with my leg and the death of my child. I would sit in the front living room with a picture of my baby lying in her coffin, which my baby brother took in order to remember her birth. My family did not tell me about the picture and they forgot to put it away before I came home from the hospital. When I saw the picture, I broke down and cried and for a whole year, I sat for hours staring at it. My family did not know that I was mentally having a nervous break down because I had learned to play everything off as if it was okay. I did not go anywhere, I dropped out of college, and I had nothing to do with men anymore for almost that entire year.

A friend of mine from Jones Jr. College came by to visit me and he noticed that I was not myself and his comments to me was, "Are you going to continue to sit here and give up on yourself, or are you going to get your life back"? He said to me that he understood my pain because he too had a child to die at birth and that he and his girlfriend went through the same thing I was going through, he said but we cried out to God for help and He strengthen us to make it one day at a time. I cried and cried in his arms and I felt some relief because God had sent someone to minister to my pain. No one noticed that I was dying in myself and that I did not know how to deal with it, but God saw my pain and sent someone to help me. I bounced back from that depression stage, met another person, went on a date with him, started trying to smoke cigarettes, trying to fit in with the crowd, and got pregnant by this person in January of 1983. I found out later that this person had something to do with my brother's death and it was as if my life was going around in circles. It was like when I would bounce back from one thing in my life something

else would take a hole. It seemed as though God was saying
something to me but I was not getting it. I felt like the children
of Israel when they were wandering around in the wilderness for
forty years.

•CHAPTER THREE•

Life as an Adult

I gave birth to my second son on October 30, 1983. I did not return to College at all after that. With two children and still living with my parents, I had to go back to work full-time. I work at Collins poultry plant for over a year and a half when I met this person from Prentiss, MS. I told him about my struggles and how I wanted to be on my own since I had two children and needing to be out of my parent's house. He offered to help me find a place; he spent time with my children and helped me to move into my new apartment. I was on section 8, so I did not need him to help me with my money situation and I think that was what drew him to me because he saw me as an independent woman. I knew how to survive and how to make a living for myself because my Dad had taught us how to work for what we wanted out of life.

Whatever we learned at the crucial age in our lives, which is 0 to 6 years of age, will follow us the rest of our lives weather they be positive things or negative things. Most importantly, if we do not allow God to come in to mold and shape us into His Will, we will let those things cause us to be less than what God has created us to be. I thank God for my Dad teaching me how to work for what I wanted and my mother for teaching that in life that whatever I desire I can have in Jesus' Name according to God's Will. My parents helped me a great deal in the things I was taught and in the rearing of my children so I did not have to have a man or a sugar daddy to help me. The problems I were having were wanting to be loved for me and not for what I had to contribute to other folk, including my family; even with all the love my family was giving me, there was something missing in my life and I was looking for it in men.

Finally this guy moved in with me for a few months and things began to get out of hand; he was having problems with an ex girlfriend and she was starting junk with me, and I did not want to deal with that; I had enough problems of my own. The one thing that my friend did not know about me was that whenever I was with someone, I was faithful to him. I never cheated on the man that I was in a relationship with. I treated our relationship as if it was a marriage; I took ownership over someone that was not mine.

As I think back over the relationships I have had in my lifetime, I am reminded of the fact that I was involved with another woman's husband, because those people that I was involved with were not the soul mate that God had for me. Another thing that I did not share with my boyfriend was my feelings toward my Dad and my first child's Dad, which I knew, was the soul-mate that God had for me. The two most important men in my life had hurt me and nothing else or no one else mattered to me. I would have married this person from Prentiss, because he reminded me so much of Doc. He was tall like him, had the same kind of attitude about himself as Doc had. You see, I really loved Doc, but I could not continue to let Doc use me and I found myself doing the same thing to other people like what Doc had done to me. That spirit had taken control over my life through the hurt and pain I was going through. I got over the symptoms of the pain but never dealt with the pains themselves, the root of my problems. In addition, how can you deal with the root of your problems when you are not sure what is the problem.

My oldest child was six years old when Doc finally owned up to being his Dad. I had just broken up with the person from Prentiss, and was working on changing my life as far as men were concern. After the death of my child and the relationships I had being in, I noticed that my life had changed for the worst. From

1983 to 1985, I had three relationships with three different men within a year's time of each other. Tell me that my life was not mess up. If I were to find out that the person I was living with was cheating on me, I would drop him like a hot potato and would not think anything about it. I would move on to the next relationship in my life. No other man could take my heart and mess over it the way Doc did, so nothing matter to me. I was miserable and full of hell. I hated myself, I hated my life; I did not know who I was. I needed help and was hurting deeply but no one saw my pain but God.

Doc would come by and bring child support for our child and that would help me out a lot but I never asked those others for anything for my children. They felt the need to do for my children because they were with me. The system did sue my second son's Dad for child support, but I never sued Doc because my mother talked me out of it and because I was in love with him. I loved Doc so much that if he had told me to jump off the nearest bridge, I would have tried to do so knowing that I could not swim a lick. I just could not say no to him to save my life except to lie to him about our child. May be if I had told him the truth about our little girl, my life would have being different, and maybe not because this man had me wrapped around his finger in knots. I was so control by him that it made me sick.

In 1986, with the help of both the child support money coming in and my new job in Prentiss and Sonic Drive-in, I managed to have some stability in my life. I worked hard to get off welfare but continue to get food stamps with my mind set on getting off them as well; but I new it would take time. Also in 1986, I applied for a low-income home and was approved but I needed $600.00 for a down payment, so I asked Doc to give me the money, he did so and I moved into my new home that same year.

In the summer of 1987, Doc came by and posed a question to me that left me speechless and in the mist of all of that he never bother to tell me that he had devoiced his first wife and was in a relationship with someone else. He never told me that he had a child by this woman he was now in a relationship with at this point, nor did he bother to tell me that he had a child by another woman as well. He wanted me to let him move in with me because the woman he was living with was giving him hell. He brought his child with him that day and posed that question to me; I looked at him as if to say what do you expect me to do. All I could see in front of me was that child and rationalized in my spirit that if there is a child, there had to be a woman somewhere. I could not say anything to him at that point, so he just said to me that he would give me a chance to think about his proposal and left. One thing about Doc, he never pushed his way, he would just leave you in a state of wonder.

On the other hand, there had being this person bugging me to go on a date with him and I was not interested in being with anyone. I had gotten my life headed in the right direction so I thought and was not thinking about a relationship of any kind with anybody. I had made up in my mind that I was not going to date another person because I did not want to be in a relationship and I did not want to keep giving myself to sexual habits. However, when Doc posed that question to me that person really started to look good for an excuse to say I am already in a relationship with someone just to get back at him. He had did it to me again a third time but this time there was not a baby involved at least not by me. My feelings were crushed all over again. I spent countless time trying to justify why I needed to let him move in, and for the life of me, I could not do it. I could not say okay! You can move in. Finally, I was able to say no to Doc but my answer "No" had an attachment to it. My answer "No" to Doc was not just a simple "No", it was more of a "because I was in another relationship". I was stilling lying to Doc.

Doc came back for an answer to his question and I boldly told him that I was seeing someone. He accused me of lying to him because there was never anyone at my house at night. How in the world he knew that beats me. My children stayed with my parents because I worked the night shift at Prentiss Complex and sometimes, I would pull a double to have more money on hand; so I was dating this person over the phone. Because I worked all the time at night, I was not going out with him at all. I dated this person for six months while my family spent most of their time with him. This person would always spend time with my children on a daily bases. He would go out to my parents house to make sure that the children had what they needed and sometimes I would call him up to go get them for me and bring them home for the weekend because I would be tired from working all week.

I started noticing how good he was with my children and how my children cared about him. It made a difference to me for their sake. Sometimes whenever I would get home from work he would stay a little while and talk and then leave; but this particular night he decided to ask if he could stay. I told him sure and it went from that one night of staying over, sleeping on the sofa to more nights of staying and then actually ended up shacking together for about a year with him constantly asking me to marry him. I knew that I could not marry this man because even though I loved him in a special way, I was not in love with him as I was with Doc and he was too nice to my children and to me for me to hurt him. I never wanted to hurt anyone the way Doc had hurt me. I purposed that in my heart because that pain of hurt caused me to lose myself in reality and I did not want that to happen to anyone else and I did not want to end up being the cause of this man's pain. However, when I saw that this person was getting serious about me, I really tried to end the relationship because I truly was not in love with him. I cared about him deeply and loved him but was not in love with him.

This man asked me three times to marry him and I kept saying no; and in order to stop him from asking me I finally told him that the only way I would marry him would be that I came up pregnant. May of 1989, I ended up pregnant with my third son by this man and I remember thinking to myself did I speak this ordeal on myself? We got married three months later, which was August of 1989. The whole time I am going though this wedding process my heart was not in it. My best friend was my maid of honor and I remember calling her into one of the bedrooms in our home to tell her that I could not go though with this; but both our families were there, friends were there and I could not stop it. It was too late. It was now time for my Dad to walk me down the ail and the whole time I'm walking there is this still voice whispering to me saying that this is not your husband, but because I did not want to leave this man at the alter of marriage I went through it anyway.

The most important reason I went fort with this marriage was that I had vowed to myself that I would not have another child out of wedlock and another part of it was because I did not want to hurt this man, the father of my child the same way Doc had hurt me. I kept seeing the same patterns in my life over and repeatedly. I had so much hatred and love for Doc that it clouded my thinking and my heart went out to a man that I was about to marry for the wrong reasons.

The first couple of years of our marriage were fine until one day I started noticing his mood-swings changing from one extreme to another. He had always drank alcohol, even though I did not mention it in the above lines, but his drinking seemed to had gotten worse and he would always say things like I know you still love that Negro. I had no idea of what he was talking about and I would not allow myself to think about what he was talking about anyway. I had buried my feelings so deep under the surface of my heart that I never thought about them until one day Doc came by the house to get his son. Those old feelings started to surface all over again. I had managed to hide my feelings as long as I did not see Doc; as long as I was not around him. After he left, my spouse began to throw a fit because my child's dad came by the house to pick him up. One thing I knew about my ex-husband was that he was crazy about my children. He never made any difference in them; they were his children and that was that. I will always have great respect for him just for the way he treated my children. There is not another person that had influenced my first two children's lives with love the way this man had and I will always hole such high respect toward him for that act of love.

During all of this time, I had had my fourth son in May of 1993, which my due date was to be February 20, the same date that my little girl was born. I was terrified that something was going to happen to my unborn child as it did with her and something did happen with him. He was born with yellow junta and had to stay in the hospital at Forrest General for over a week and he would stay sick all the time. It had not dawn on me that whatever I thought about, it would happen. I had not realized that there was power in my thinking. To keep down confusion in my home, my spouse at the time would ask me to tell Doc to pick our child up at my mom's house and I did so for peace sake. After that ordeal had calm down a little, my older son began bringing things into the house that his Dad would buy for him and my spouse would throw a fit about that. I truly believe that that is when my spouse began to deal in drugs, as we will see in the chapters to come. His older brother was already a major seller so that was all he needed to get started; he had the connection that he needed. He felt less of a man because he could not buy the things he wanted his family to have, and seeing a man that I once knew and loved was buying these great things for our children that he could not buy caused him to become envious of Doc and he began taking his frustration out on me. He even said to me a number of times that he wanted his family to have the best and that he will do whatever it took to give it to us.

Therefore, I spent my entire life running from a man that I truly loved and ending up marring a man that truly loved my children and me; but who I was not in love with. Whenever Doc wanted to be with me, I did not want to be with him; and whenever I wanted to be with Doc, he did not want to be with me. We were back and forth in our relationship with each other; therefore, both our lives were mess up and we are still mess up to a point in some areas of our lives even now that we are together. Therefore, this is where my relationship began as far as the crushing process with the Lord. I had come through some rough times and would endure more as I proceed through what I called a journey to destiny. *My life as a chosen Prophetess of God.*

•CHAPTER FOUR•

Call to a Relationship with God

B efore I explain to you what the meaning of the crushing process is, let me share with you what really brought me here to this crushing process. I was going through some hard times in my life. First, I had children out of wedlock by my high school sweetheart, had multiple relationships, got married in 1989, had my third child in 1990, was in an abusive marriage, became very suicidal, and wanted desperately to end my life all together. There was never mornings that I would drive to work without thinking about killing myself. Born and raised in the church for thirty years and ending up walking away from the one person who could help me through all the things I was going through for three years "God" my Heavenly Father.

In 1994, I return to the church during the first week of April. I can remember it so well because it was the turning point of my life. It was on a Thursday night of our church revival while I was sitting in the very back of the church. I can't tell you what the message was about or where the minister was coming from in his text, all I know is that during the alter call, I stood up at my seat with tears rolling down my face. Calling out to God to help me please and at that moment I remember something felt as if it rested on my shoulders. Every problem I was going through had left my mind and caused me to focus on that touch.

The next morning driving to work, I forgot about suicide; my mind was on what had happened to me at church. There was this young woman at work that knew the Lord and all I could think in my mind was that I needed to get to this person. When I got to work that morning I waited for the young woman to come in so that I could tell her what had happened to me in hopes that she could explain it to me.

The young woman final came in and I was all over her with high expectations that she could explain my experience. After telling her what had happened to me, she says to me well sometimes the devil will sit on you to keep you from going up, and I said going where? She says to the Altar. In that instance, I realized that her mind was focus on going up front to except Christ. I stated to her, No! I know that that was not the devil because if I did not know anything else about the Spirit of the Lord, I knew something about the devil and his mess especially with all the hell I was going through.

So I just kept thinking about that experience as I went through my day, when later on the young lady came back to me and invited me to go to church with her the following Sunday. Due to the fact that my husband had beaten me down so in my spirit physical and verbally, my first thoughts was no I better not go, but there were something inside of me said to say yes. Therefore, I told her yes I will go and for some reason I could not wait to get there. I did not know at that time that I would be separating from my husband. I left him that very same weekend. Note that I said I left my husband, not that God told me to leave. I need to make that point clear because later on you will understand why I have made this statement.

Sunday morning finally came and I went to my home church first because the young woman was not picking me up until two O'clock that evening. After my friend picked me up, there was this book lying on the seat and I promise you that book started talking to me in my spirit. Benny Hinn wrote this book and he called the name of this book "Good Morning Holy Spirit". I tried hard not to say anything about it to my friend, but the more I tried to ignore it something kept saying you need this book to read. Therefore, I turned to my friend and said, something is telling me that I need to read this book. I do not know why but it keeps telling me I need this book. My friend began to say to me she had just brought the book to read herself, but she let me take the book anyway.

Finally, we got to the church, which was a little old woman's house where some mission women would meet after they had attended their home churches. During that time the enemy brought a thought to my mind that my daddy would always tell me, stay away from those places where people meet in houses and call it a church. My mind was racing with thoughts of that but I was so desperate for answers to what was going on with me that I looked past that thought.

The minute we arrived in the driveway, this woman came out on the porch, looked at me, and said this woman came here looking for something and God has your answer here today. Now this woman had never seen me, I had never seen her; she did not know me from Adam. I knew it had to be something or somebody that was bringing this about because you must understand that at this point I did not know the Holy Spirit, had not being taught in the things of the Holy Spirit, but He was very much active in my life through all of this.

As we entered into service, the ladies that were there began testifying to the goodness of the Lord, which I didn't know what it was called at the time because I had not being exposed to it before. They began standing up sharing what God had done in their lives and how He was doing it and I remember saying to myself I do not have anything to say in reference to what the others were saying. Therefore, I said I'd just say what they are saying and move on. It was my turn to speak and so I stood up to repeat what the others had said when something took complete control of my mouth and said what was in my heart. When I knew anything, I hit the floor and by the time I got up off the floor, my life had changed just that quickly. I knew I was a changed person and that I was not the same person that I was before I walked into that house.

I went back home with the book "Good Morning Holy Spirit" in my hands and Jesus Christ in my heart as Lord. I had being saved for years but had not made Jesus Lord of my life. We can be saved all of our lives but until we invite the Lord to take full control of our lives, we will never experience the Power of the living

God. My Daddy looked at me with amazement and said girl what in the world has happened to you. You are not the same person that left here some hours ago. You have the Glory of God shinning through you. What happened? I looked at my Daddy and said, Daddy! God has given me a new attitude and a new walk. I could not begin to explain to him what had happened to me; all I knew was that I went down on the floor, got back up a changed person.

The next day I began reading the book and what I encountered in this book was that God had already prepared me with a tool that would teach me how to walk in the Spirit of Him, the Holy Spirit. He gave me the book to teach me how to talk to Him and how to know His voice. As I read the book, the more things began to make sense to me. All the times that I was saying something told me, or something touched me, it was the Holy Spirit; and what God was saying I have being with you all the time, you just got lost in your circumstances and forgot about me.

God said to me, "You are now ready to allow me to be Lord of your life, and because you have finally come to that point, "This is where I am taking you and this is who I am calling you to be in my plan. I am calling you to the Office of a Prophet. You have heard me speaking to you through signs and wonders, but you have not understood what I was doing. Now that I have shown you who

you are in Me, I want you to know that this journey is going to be a

lonely trip, but if you stay with Me (God) you can make it." When

He spoke that to me, I was like Moses. I started making all kinds

of excuses to why I could not do what He was calling me to do. My

spirit was willing to accept what He was speaking to me but my flesh

was weak and I mean very weak. I was afraid to let God be God in

my life. I was afraid of the unfamiliar territory that God was about

to take me through.

•CHAPTER FIVE•

Call to walk in a Death Walk with God

After God said to me that He was calling me to the Office of a Prophet, things out of the ordinary started really happening and it was worst than when He was speaking to me. The first manifestation I had from God was a called from Benny Hinn himself. I was sowing a seed into his ministry because his book was blessing me. I was also sowing a seed into a church that was not my home church; and somehow the checks were mailed to the wrong places. Benny Hinn called me to tell me, which I thought was ironic because normally their secretary would handle that for them.

Later on that night, I had a dream about death. In that dream the devil was telling me you are going to die, and all I could think of was a physical death. It never entered my mind that it was a spiritual death walk, dying to my self-will for God's will. Satan always wants us to think of the worst in situations. I wrestled with that thought for days and God never revealed to me what it all meant; and I cannot remember ever asking Him to reveal it because I was afraid of the answer. I was not ready to die a physical death.

This walk of death in which I did not understand came mightily after God sent me back home to my abusive spouse. I can remember it so clearly; when God said, it is now time to go home. I said to God, "Lord please no, I'm happy the way I am now; but He said to me again, "Go home." As I prepared to go back to my spouse, very reluctant to go; the first night I get home he jumps on me; and I remember saying, "God is this what you sent me back for, for this man to abuse me all over again?" I said to God, "I rather die than be here in this mess." All God would say to me was "My grace is sufficient for you," which again I did not understand where He was coming from with that statement. You must remember that I was learning to walk with Him. Therefore, not everything was clear to me in this stage of my death walk.

The next day I was thinking over everything in my head, looking at how happy I was before I went back to my husband. How I was feeling like I was defeated all over again. I could not understand why God brought me back into this situation. He was not telling me anything except "My grace is sufficient." Even though God was not saying that much to me, I continue to lone for Him, which went on for days at a time. Then one day I was watching Christian television and this minister was talking about the situation I was going through. One of the things that he said was that God is allowing you to go through this ordeal because He is trying to teach you about unconditional love. Something in my spirit connected to that statement and I began to seek God the more for clarity.

The more I talked to God about my situations and the statement of unconditional love, God spoke and said to me "would you love your husband in spite of how he is treating you, will you be willing to go through the fire that I am about to take you through. Are you willing to go through in spite of the things others will say and do because this walk will cause you to die to yourself and your ways"? I was so glad to hear God speak to me again until the Holy Spirit moved me to say, ""Yes Lord!"

•CHAPTER SIX•

Test of Unconditional Love with God

After saying Yes Lord to God's test of unconditional love, everything in my household began to crumble. I found out my spouse at the time was selling drugs, cheating on me, and having babies while we were still together; you name it, it was happening in my life.

Suspecting that my spouse was doing all of the above especially the drug selling, I set out to expose his hidden secrets. I knew something was going on in that area because of the heavy trafficking that was going on in and out of my house late at night. Trying to expose whatever was going on, I would sit up at night trying to see in the dark with all the lights out to catch him, would call the police whenever I would come home from work to find a host of people coming out of my house. You see, when you care

for someone you do not condom the wrong that they do especially

when you are a child of God; I called it true love for a lost soul.

One of us had to have some sense about moral and values. We had

children that needed us to rear them in the admonition of the Lord

just as the Bible had stated and by me being the spiritual leader

in the home God was going to hold me responsible for what was

happening just as He did with Eli and his sons.

Sometimes we as believers have to challenge a person in

order to rescue him or her from himself or herself, even if it means

calling the law on them. Whenever I would question my spouse

about his activities, he would accuse me of cheating on him with

my dad, my pastor, my brothers, or any man I would meet. I would

call out to God for help and again God would say, "My Grace is

sufficient for you."

As I grew in the Lord more and more, things began to

happen to me. God began to speak to me the more about witnessing

to the very people my spouse was selling drugs too. I remember

that one day God said He is going to send me in the mist of those

people to share the gospel with them; how much He loved them and

why they needed to get their lives together with Him. I thought to

myself God! You have got to be kidding me. I know you are not telling me to jeopardize my family's lives in that way. God spoke to me and said, "Lo I am with you always, even until the ends of the earth." I said God you have got to be kidding me.

God kept telling me to do as He has commanded me to do until I finally did what He said. After my spouse came home from work that evening, his friends had informed him of what I had done; he came to me fussing about it. His words were, "Are you trying to get us killed?" Those people think that you are a narcotic agent. They are saying that you are working for the cops; but for some reason it did not bother me what the people were thinking. I felt at peace after doing what God had instructed me to do.

The next test of faith was God taking me into trances, which were more like out of body experiences. I was able to see into the Spiritual rim of God. One day I was sitting on the sofa when I heard the doorbell ring. It was my Mother-in-Law at the time coming through the door. As I looked at her, I could see evil-spirits all around her and I immediately began to plead the Blood of Jesus over myself. I could see the devil in her eyes. She had the strangest look on her face as she looked at me. After so long, she and my spouse walked outside and I noticed that they were walking around the house several times. It did not dawn on me that the devil was setting a trap for me until strange things started happening; things that was so blizzard that I knew something was not right. My ex mother-in-law would always go to the homes of fortune-tellers for advice, so I thought to myself that what ever spirits that those people were possessing had a toll on her as well and I was afraid of what I was seeing.

I can remember one night that God led me to get out of bed and go into prayer. I remember trying to be quiet so that I would not wake my spouse in the mist of my praying and as I began to pray, the Spirit of the Lord got stronger and stronger on me until I began to see in the spirit that my spouse was standing in the living room close by. I felt him move closer to me and then walk away. I then heard the water running in the kitchen sink. I felt him move toward me again because all of this time my eyes are closed and the house is dark; there were no lights on during this time. The next thing I knew the water he had gotten from the kitchen sink was now in my face, but I kept on praising God in spite of what my spouse was doing. Sometimes we have to keep on keeping on no matter what it feels like or looks like, we have to continue to trust God.

At that point, God spoke to me to continue to keep my eyes closed. Right after God had spoken those words to me, I felt and tasted salt in my face and mouth. This man said to me that somebody had hoodooed you and it is getting out of here tonight. Right when he said that an audible voice spoke through me and said, "She is not of the devil; she is my child, touch not my anointed and do my prophet no harm." I went to the bathroom to wash my face and when I came back into the living room my spouse stood with a look on his face as to say what was that, and little did he know I was just as shocked and scared as he was. He took the word scared right out of my mouth when he said, "You thought that scared me, but it did not." Nevertheless, ask me did he put his hands on me again after that. In my spirit, I knew that God had spoken through me audibly and my faith grew even the more after that.

Days had gone by and there were a lot of fussing in the house from my spouse but God had given me such a joy that I was able to hold my peace in the mist of that entire ordeal he was doing. After that incident, the most promising and cleaning experience happened to me. It was on a Sunday Morning, I was to go to church somewhere but I was not sure where God was telling me to go and He defiantly was not telling me to go to my home church. My home church was not ready for what God was doing with me and I could not explain what was going on either. As I prepared to get dress to leave, I went into another trance and this time it seemed more like a ceremonial type service because my third child, which was six at the time, was in the guest bedroom putting things in a circle, he was moving in such slow motion that it was strange. I had learned to charge everything that was strange or out of the ordinary to God.

After watching him for a minute or two, I sat down on the sofa and began to talk to God about what He was showing me. He would lead me to go and finish getting dress to leave for church; and as I would go toward the tub to bathe, I could not step into the water. Something would stop me at the door. I did not understand what was happening. Finally, getting into the tub was behind me; I could hear the voice of God saying washed in His Blood. Every time I would wash myself, I could hear those words, so I knew that it was a baptism-taking place in my tub.

My bath experience was over; I was dressed and started out the door and could not go through the door. My thoughts were here we go again. I felt as though something was trying to keep me from leaving my house. At that point, my spouse was so worried about me that he began to say to me what in the world is wrong with you. Why are you acting like this? I said to him I do not know, I need some help. I don't know where I'm supposed to go; I don't know what I'm supposed to do; please take me to Elaine's house who was my friend and sister in Christ, maybe she can tell me something. When we got to her house she was not there and I said to my spouse maybe she went to the church up the street from her house. The Church up the street was a Holiness Church that my friend once belonged to and I knew that there were strange movements of God taking place there, and I would not have being out of place there for what God was doing in my life. After all of those years, I now understand why God sent me to that Church. I never knew the reason until now year 2005. Praise God!

As we started up the street toward the church, God spoke to me and said, "I have an angle waiting for you on the porch at the church and just as He spoke those words to me, this woman dressed in white was pacing the porch. My spouse pulls up to the church and says to the woman, "My wife is acting strange and she asked me to bring her here; will you please take care of her? In addition, the woman answered and said, "We sure will because we have being waiting for her."

When the woman and I walk into the church, everything that was happening at my house was taking place in that church. The vision of a man dressed in a white rode with a grass rope tied around him standing in front of the congregation, just as I had seen in the vision at home; He was preparing for the Lord's Supper. The Pastor began to tell the people that we are going to come around the communion table a little different from how we normally would do. He stated that what he wanted everyone to do was to take every three pews and march around in a circle and come forth just like the circles that my son was making in the guest bedroom at my house. I freaked out at that moment. Therefore, I began to listen closely to what God was saying to me because I knew at that point that it was a divine appointment ordained by God Himself.

After service, I went to the woman who was waiting on the porch for me to see if she knew anything of what was going on. As I began to tell her what was happening, she says to me you need to talk to my Pastor's wife. She called the Pastor's wife over to me and I told her the story, she then too says to me you need to talk to my husband. Therefore, she went to her husband and said something to him about my situation. He called me into his office and the first thing he said to me was it sounds like someone has bewitched you with everything you have told my wife. While he was talking and taking off his robe, God spoke to me and said that everyone that knows Me (God) have not being where I am taking you because it is a supernatural experience with Me (God).

When God says a supernatural experience with Him, it is every bit that. I thought I was loosing my mind. Things were happening so fast that it was like a whirlwind spending round and around. I was seeing the devil and his vices face to face. My dear mother thought that I was Wit Field bound. Strange stuff was happening so often to me, until one day, I had gone to pick my mother up from work and while we were riding down the highway, I stopped in the middle of it and screamed to the top of my lungs "Jesus" so loud that Satan loosed his fight over my life. From that day to now, I have being walking in the presence of the Lord. I chose that day to walk with God. The Word of God tells us to choose ye this day whom you will serve because we can not serve to masters. The devil still shows up in my life today but I have learned how to say Jesus with authority. The word of God declares that if we resist the devil he will flee from us. What God was doing was maturing my faith in Him. I grew and grew in the knowledge and revelation of His Word after that ordeal.

All of this was taking place in 1994. I was working with a company that made car harness for eight years. During the time, I was going though these experiences, God had promoted me to head utility over the line. An assembly line consisted of thirteen stations. I had to learn all thirteen stations as well as play the roll of an active supervisor whenever the supervisor would be out. I can remember that one day I was at the end of one of the stations on the line when all of a sudden I heard this beautiful music playing in my ear. I turn to the young woman standing next to me to ask her if she had heard the music. She replied to me what music and I immediately said okay God this has to be you. It was such a beautiful melody playing in my ear that cause me to be caught up in the atmosphere of heaven. I could hear God saying to me through the music that it was time to fly away.

•CHAPTER SEVEN•

Call to Trust God

In 1995, I was up for another promotion on my job as head supervisor over the line that I was working on already; but God said not on this job. He said to me to resign from the company. Everyone thought I was crazy for resigning when I was up for a promotion to make more money. However, when you are working for the Lord, then our time is not our time; it is God's time so you learned to walk in obedience to what God says. I left in 1995 just as God had instructed me to do and I did not work for six months. When He (God) released me to go back to work, I went in a total different direction than what I was accustomed to doing. I had always worked on factory jobs, but this time God sent me into the nursing field working with elderly people. I worked in nursing homes in Covington County and two in Hattiesburg for a couple of years.

Also in 1995, my spouse started acting up with me again and this time it was more than the drugs. I was hearing more and more about him cheating on me, and the babies he was birthing out of these relationships. In fact, one of the women he was having the affair with was working on a part-time job with me. What was so interesting to me was that God revealed to me that she was one of his women and I was not brother by the information. I would always ask God for information concerning anything that I needed to know about life's situations and so forth. I treated the woman with the utmost respect. The people that worked with us would always say to me how can you befriend someone who is going with your husband? My reply would always be they are the ones with the problem because they will have to answer to God. I was responsible for my actions and I did not want to mess up my relationship with God. I knew soon or later God was going to handle the situation. My coworkers just could not believe what was going on with me.

My spouse infidelity got so bad that he would not come home some nights and when he did come home, he would always be drunk. Every time he came home drunk, he would want to fight, which I found out later that he did that so he could stand up against me if I fussed about him not coming home. I never said a word and that killed him more than anything did. I can remember one participle night he came home high and the devil had him so pumped up that he wanted to take me out of this world. He jumped on everybody that was in the house. I picked up the phone and called the police; when he heard me on the phone, he took the phone from me and threw me on the sofa, hit me a few times and ran down the hall, came back with a gun in his hand. He put the gun next to my head and said I will kill you "B", and tried hard to get the safety latch off but God did not allow him to succeed. He dropped the gun and he took off running out the door.

When the police finally got to my home, I began to tell them what had happened and they patrol the area but could not find him. Later on in the wee hours of the morning, I could see him trying to ease back into the house, so I called the police again and they came and took him away. I just knew that God was going to release me from that marriage after all of that, but He did not say anything.

I knew that when my spouse got out of jail he was coming back home. Therefore, I prayed hard that God would not let that be so. I kept praying and praying but God said nothing to me. The day he got out of jail, the police informed him that if he came near the house without my permission, he would have charges filed against him for assault with a deadly weapon. He took their advice and did not come near the house for a couple of days. He called to see if he could come home and a major part of my inner being was screaming no, but God was saying yes.

Now I really started seeing the reality of trusting God in unconditional love. If this was not the real deal then I did not want to see what the real thing was going to be. I knew deep down inside of me that there had to be something worst than that coming my way because this man had threaten my life and God was saying take him back.

Weeks went by and more things happened. Everything this man was going through; he still did not see what God was doing in his life. All I could do was hold my peace and show him love. God still had me to be a wife to him. It got to the point that I did not think about the things he had done to me or was doing to me because all I could focus on was what God was doing. I realized that I was suffering for Christ sake; I knew that in order for me to know him in the power of His resurrection, I had to suffer with Him; I had to learn to trust Him.

Again, this man abused me and I just could not take any

more. I purposed in my heart that I was going to leave him finally, my house and everything. You see, I wanted him to leave because the house was mine; I was buying my home and I did not want to leave it. However, that was not what God was saying to me. God was saying to me give up everything if I was going to follow Him and until I could do that God did not allow me to leave. My children spoke to me that night and said mommy we need to get out of this after he jumped on me again. I knew it had to be a word from the Lord coming from my children and I listened to their spoken words.

The next morning, which was on a Tuesday, he had gone to work so I packed clothes for the children and myself; I waited until two o'clock to leave to go to my mother's house. I wanted my Dad to be gone to work so that he would not be there to question me on what was happening, which I believe was really God's plan. Right at two O'clock, I heard a lot of commotion going on outside in the street. All of a sudden, the police officers push their way into my home. They began to talk to me like I was not human saying sit down and do not move. I sat there on the sofa and watched them ram sack my house looking for drugs. It was a drug bust going down in my home and all I could do was pray to God. Everything I had suspected was going on was now a reality in my life and in my home. I cried out to God for help. The Cops were coming out with all sorts of stuff this man had stashed away in our home. I could not believe what I was seeing.

I knew it was a set up ordained by God because I found out later that my spouse had not intended to leave his stashed there that morning so that was why I was not able to find anything to catch him on because he would come home late at night while I was in the bed sleep. He would take his stuff with him when he would leave for work the next morning.

One of the Cops said to me to get up and help search for stuff that maybe in the house and I said I have no idea what I'm looking for because this man has being lying to me concerning his illegal activities and the cop said look anyway because that will help you out. I thought to myself how that would help me out when I have not done anything. The Holy Spirit spoke to me to get up and do what the officer ask me to do.

After the search was over the cops came and said to me because you help us out and you had being calling us concerning what you thought was going on, we are not going to take you or the children downtown because we feel strongly that you did not have anything to do with your husband's activities. I said to God I thank you Lord for being faithful to your word because it came back to me what God had told me in the beginning that it will all be over after while. When God said that to me I did not understand at that moment but it all began to come together in that situation.

God had released me from the hands of the devil. I left my house that same day to never to return. My children and I moved out to my mom's house until I could find somewhere for us to stay. We gave up a three bedroom, brick home for a two bedroom, wooden house out in the woods but we were happy once again.

•CHAPTER EIGHT•

Putting My Life Back Together with God

After all of the things that had gone down in my life, it was time now to piece my life back together with the help of the Lord. I had grown mightily in God through faith and trust in Him that there was nothing to whole me back from going where God was taking me. God had released me from an abusive husband and the life he was living and brought me into a wealthy place with Him. I was able to spend a lot of time with Him and really get into church more and His Word.

In 1996, God led me to go back to school at Jones Jr. College, which I had attended in 1978 after graduating from high school. I majored in Childcare and Development and was an honor student until I got a bright ideal that I wanted to work a full-time job at night and go to school full-time in the day. I would work the eleven to seven shifts all night at Ellisville State School and would leave there and go to Jones for an eight O'clock class that morning.

Everything that I had gone through was the beginning of God calling me to the ministry. The call was to preach with a stronger calling to the office of a Prophet as well. I went for days not understanding God's call to preach because I was a woman and had being told all of my life and had come to believe that God don't call women to preach His word. There were many times I had gone to my Pastor to talk to him about what God was calling me to do and all he would say to me was sister whatever God is calling you to do He (God) will make it plain to you.

Therefore, in my waiting for God to make it plain to me I was ministering in areas that I were not exposed to, knew nothing about, but God was teaching me left to right. The enemy would come back to me with the fact that I was going to die soon because I was growing too fast. God blessed me with the gift of laying on of hands to heal, delivered, cast out demons and everything. The enemy again came to me and said you see you are preparing to get out of this world quick. At that moment, I thought more and more about what the enemy was saying and found myself trying to slow down my growth in God.

However, the more I grew in God's grace the more the enemy fought me. I can remember one day I was at work at Sonic Drive-In when my Ex had brought my oldest son to get some information that he needed from me because he was trying to get his driving license. About 1:30 in the afternoon, I had gotten off work and was lying down across my bed taking a nap when the phone ranged. It was someone from the hospital calling to inform me of my child being in a car accident. I perceived to ask the person where was he because I had just seen him a few hours ago with his stepfather. The person on the other end of the phone began to tell me that he was thrown out of the car and that I needed to get there fast to release them to work on him. They had him stabilized but that I need to sign some paper.

As I was driving to the hospital, I kept thinking God what is happening with my family. Is he going to be all right? God assured me that he was gong to be fine but I was not sure what I was going to find when I got to the hospital. A nurse met me at the door and took me to him; when I walked into the emergency room where he was I saw a neck brace around his neck and the nurse must have seem the expression on my face that said "oh no! he's broken his neck" because at that moment he said no he has not broken his neck it is just a precaution that we use to ensure that they have not broken their neck.

After my son realized that I was there, he looked at me as if to say I am in trouble now because Ma had told me to stay off the back roads just in case something happened. When I saw the look on his face, I knew that he felt convicted in his spirit for disobeying my orders. The one thing that really got me after all the shock of the accident was when the hospital staff was telling me that some woman had pulled him out of the middle of the road because he was thrown out of the car before it hit a tree and caught a fire.

Therefore, I began to search for this woman but no one knew who she was or had seen her after the accident. I called the police station to inquire about the accident in hopes that they could give me the name of this woman who had saved my son's life. They did not have a name of the woman nor did they have a report of the accident on file. I knew immediately that God had sent a guarding angle to watch over my child through this ordeal. My son had suffered a broken leg, a broken collarbone and a report from the doctors that said he would never play basketball the remaining of his high school years.

A week had gone by and my son was released from the

hospital that Friday evening. I got him home and put him in my bed to recover and heal. We had to help him in and out of the bed whenever he needed help and once I got him all settle down for the night I curled up on the sofa and went to sleep. It would always seem like God was speaking to me every single night for over two or three months. That particular night God was speaking to me to laid hands on my son's leg. I got right up and did what I was instructed to do after which I went back and laid down. The next morning when I woke up, my son was coming out of the bedroom, walking on a broken leg that had a pin in it without his crutches. I began to praise God for what He was doing through me.

After all of what had happened with my son and the doctor's report the devil ended up being a lie because my son did play basketball again the remaining of his high schools years, walked on campus of Jones Jr. College, and received a scholarship to play on the College team. You see what the doctors did not know but the devil did was that I was walking with a God that said I could have whatever I ask in the name of Jesus and I believed for my son's healing and God did just that and more.

Separated from my husband, growing in God and seeing the world through the eyes of God, dreams and visions started happening with me and my spirit would connect with my Pastor's spirit to understand what God had to say to me in the Spirit through my Pastor without him ever opening his mouth to tell me anything.

I became a Sunday school teacher for the Adult Women Class and later was asked to be president of the Choir. I taught a Women of God class and was the teacher of the Mission society. Therefore, you see God was preparing me for Kingdom building at a fast paste in my Christian walk.

One night at choir rehearsal we were singing this song called "Anointing fall on me" and the more we sang that song the stronger the anointing fell in the building. God led me to get the oil from the pulpit and anoint everything and everybody in the sanitary.

As we sang and anointed everybody, God began to slang people in the Spirit and others spoke in tongues; He had me to lay hands on this woman and she hit the floor; then He had me to prophesy to another woman about some things in her life concerning this person she was planning to marry etc. The young woman began to confirm that God had given me the prophecy to tell her; she said to me I know that word was from God because He had spoken that to me, she hugged me and said thank you for being obedient to the voice of God. After she left out of the room, I fell to my knees and cried out to God to teach me how to use what

He had put in me because I was afraid of what was happening. News of that night spread all over the community and people were saying things that confirmed that they knew that God was moving in my life, that there were something different about Mrs. Magee. I thought to myself what was so different about me that others felt inferior to me.

I was really bother by that statement because I knew that God had no respect of persons, that what He would do for one, He would also do for others and it really bothered me because people began to treat me different and I felt so left out. That night did not seem to me that God was just using me, but all of us to do a work for him, and somehow I got single out from the others. Church folks began to come against me and I did not understand that at all. When you talk about having being hurt by church folks, you have really gone through something. I will never forget that experience.

However, it also taught me that no matter what you go through it is all to the glory of God and that makes it all worthwhile to go through.

God then had the Pastor of the Church to put together a mini revival, which was to be the climax of the Women Day Program for all the called out women to speak. It was a three-night revival and all the speakers had three minutes to deliver a message. I tried everything I could to be the last person to speak and I ended up being on the first night, which was no that Wednesday night. However, I did manage to be the last one to speak that night. There were two speakers for each night except Friday night and that Sunday evening.

I remember God having to stop me in my tracks to let me know that He was in charge of His own program. In addition, when He finished using me that night, I took off running in the sanitary and God blessed me with a DANCE in my feet. My feet took off as if they had a mind of their own. I could not stop my feet and whenever I would lift my hands to God in surrender to Him, things would happen. Praise would come from my soul like never before and it got worse and worse that I could not control it. Whenever I would think of what God had brought me through, my soul, my very being would worship Him like no other force. I was label the runner by church folks but it did not bother me because nobody knew what God was doing for me and in me.

Afterwards, my Pastor got up and explained to the congregation about what God was doing with me. He explained the reason God had stopped me in the middle of the message. He told them that whenever God has His hands on an individual then that person can't do what he or she wants to do, but that I was under the leading and the guiding of God Almighty and that nothing I do would prosper outside of God's Will for my life. I was given charge by my Pastor that night to preach the Word of God.

On that Friday night, the mother of the church spoke and while she was speaking, one of the young women who had spoken that Thursday night fell out with a seizer and God spoke to me to observe what was taken place because He was teaching me how to use the Gift of laying on of hands. Therefore, I began to pay attention to what was going on as the other women who had being exposed to that kind of thing worked with the young woman. After everything was over and we all had gone home that night, I thought about everything that took place. I spent all day that Saturday meditating on that entire three nights and realizing that God had move mightily in the body.

Early that Sunday morning around two O'clock in the wee hours of the morning, I woke up to a fiery right hand; did not know what was happening and my Pastor had told me that if I needed to call him no matter the time, to do so. He knew that God was preparing me for something that day, so I took him up on his word and called him. All God would allow him to say to me at that time was well sister whatever God is telling you to do just be obedient to His voice. I got to Church that morning, taught the Sunday School class, got prepared for morning Worship with the choir, we marched into the choir stands, sung a song, and during the devotional, my Pastor leaves the pulpit for a few minutes and when he comes back he stops and look in a direction on the other side of the Church. We all were looking at him because it is time for the Word, so we are wondering what is going on with him.

I began to question God on what was going on and by that time this lady sitting in front of me shouts out this girl's name to me and I look over into the direction in which she was pointing I noticed that the same girl that had falling out with a seizer that Friday night was down again. So I go over to where she was and bends over her; by the time I get down near her my Pastor walks over as well, so I removed myself from her allowing him to look after her due to the fact that he was her leader; all of a sudden he gets up and walks away. I said to myself where in the world is he going. At that instance, God says to me do what I have instructed you to do.

Therefore, I bend over her again to do what God had said to do. Therefore, I began to lay hands on her and the shaking ceased.

We got her up and headed out the door with her when she collapsed again. We worked with her some more and we finally got her to the women lounge where she could rest and still hear the Word of God going forth. During the service, my Pastor again explained to the congregation of what was happening with me and he made it known to the congregation that God had given me the Gift of laying on of hands, and after service was over the people flocked to me saying lay your hands on me and I was like Oh! My! God.

After the service, the young woman seem to be doing better so I went back to my post in the choir to get ready for the next service, which was the climax of the Women Day program that was getting ready to start. The young woman called me outside to ask me to sing the hymn of preparation for her because she was on program to do it. I normally would have said you can do it, but I went on and did it anyway. I rendered the hymn "Guide me O thou Great Jehovah" and as I got into the hymn, God says to me open your eyes and when I did I looked right into the face of my oldest child dad. I was like Oh! My God. I was so into praising the Lord that it did not matter to me who was sitting in the congregation and what God was doing was giving my child's dad a first hand look at who I had become. God was showing him that I was not the same person he once knew years ago.

After service that day, my child dad came up to me and said you are different from whom I remembered you. You have changed a great deal. My words were that is who Jesus is, that is how He works in the lives of his people.

A lot was taking place in my life at that time because God was getting me ready for a move. Toward the third month, which was March, the enemy was really trying to keep me down. My ex came by to see the children and I notice he kept hanging around until it was time for the kids to go to bed. I asked him to leave because I was getting ready for bed myself. It was getting late and we all had to get up for school the next morning. His reply was you go ahead and go on to bed and I will lock the door on my way out. I was not thinking that he had something else up his sleeve, I just trusted him because he was the children dad.

The next thing I knew this man was in my bedroom which resulting in him forcing himself on me. My ex had raped me and all I could do was to cry out to God in his behalf for forgiveness because my ex did not realize what he had done to me in the eyesight of God. God had warned him before not to touch His anointed and do His prophet no harm. As I began to cry out to God on behalf of my ex, God began to purge me at that very moment. So many times the enemy tricks us into doing things because we feel that we have the right to. My ex thought that he could continue to do whatever he wanted to with me without my permission. The enemy has us thinking that a Pastor, or an anointed person of God is just an ordinary person but I must warn you that they are not.

A word of warning from the Lord, if by any chance you are married to a man or woman of God and they are a Pastor of a church and you see him or her as your husband or wife in the Church in which you are a member, you are in error with God. That man or that woman is not your husband or wife at the Church, he or she is your Pastor. Everything that goes for the other members of the Church also applies to you the wife or husband of that Pastor. I just thought that I would throw that in free.

Many of us find ourselves in error with the Lord because we treat the affairs of God with no respect. We have no respect whatsoever for the things of God or His people. How can we disrespect the authority of God through His Servants? We must go back to the reverence of God Almighty

The next morning I got the kids up for school and afterwards, I prepared to leave for school as well. Classes for me was over at twelve noon everyday, so when I got to the place to turn off to go home, I noticed a group of narcotic agents with a dog in the car hanging around at the end of my street.

Again, I questioned God to what was happening. God warned me that the narcotics were watching my house. One thing about God is that He will not let anything slip upon His children and He states that in His Word. After getting home, I began to search to see if my Ex had left something lying around to set me up. Lo and behold, lying there in my bed was a bag of weed rolled up. I thought to myself that that no good devil was still trying to take me down. After that, my ex could not come by my house again.

Toward the end of April, I received a call from my oldest child dad telling me that I had better get ready because he was coming home to claim what was his. I was not trying to hear any of that and nothing else from a man especially from someone that I already knew about. My mind was on God and God alone. Weeks later I had a dream around two O'clock in the morning which was on a Thursday; in that dream I saw my ex sitting in jail, which he was in jail at the time, and Jesus was standing over him. At that instance, I woke up and God spoke to me that He was sending him home.

I wonder why I was left in a state of mind to why God would speak that to me and since the dream was dealing with my Ex; I just assume that my Ex was whom God was talking about. I had not given another thought to the phone call I had received from Doc, my oldest child dad, and I sure was not trying to hear that I would be getting back with my Ex. However, if that was what God was saying I was not going to question it. About Eight O'clock that same morning, there were a knock at my door. When I opened the door there stood my oldest child dad in the doorway and I closed the door so fast and said, "No Lord! No" not him God, not now God please! I finally opened the door just to be polite but I did not want to deal with that situation right then. My child's dad stated to me again that he would be home for good in May and that he was coming for his bride. To be honest with you, I do not even think my child's dad new what was happening with us.

Doc came home in May as he had said and started trying to put our relationship back together. My Grandmother was also going through a period of sickness during that time so much so that my Uncles and my Aunt asked me if I would move in with her to take care of her for them. I agreed to help so I moved in with her toward the end of May. My Ex spouse was released from jail at the time but was pending a hearing sometime after that, and he was working hard trying to get his family back; so a lot was really going on in my life in the summer of 1996. In June of that year, my Dad's family had their family reunion, my older sister came home for the Reunion, and we just had a great time visiting with each other. In November of that same year, during the Thanksgiving Holidays, Doc came over to invite me to spend Thanksgiving Day with him and his family. I was not looking forward to doing that because again I held fast to the fact that I was still married, which I really was using that as an excuse not to be with Doc.

I finally accepted his invitation and did spend the Holiday with him but I invited my sister to go with me. We ended up at his house in Hattiesburg after spending time with his family and one of the things my sister said to me was how in the world did you chose the devil over this angle. My sister fell in love with Doc, but she had not known the pain he had put me through and I was very hesitant with being with him. We got through that day and the next day my ex came over to see me. I could tell that there was something going on with him, but I could not put my hands on it. My brother, which was a year older than me, went out to talk to him and found out that he was to go to prison the next day and that he had over five thousand dollars to give to the children and me, but I would not take it.

As long as I suspected my ex to be involved in drugs before I actually found out, I did not accept cash money from him. He would sign his payroll check over to me every week when we lived together as husband and wife. I did not trust him and I was not going to go alone with what he was doing. Whenever I stood for something, I stood whole heartily until the end. Many people did not like me for that, but I was not living my life for people; I was living my life for God and I stood on what I believed to be the truth, which was the Word of God. I did not condemn him for how he was living his life, but I did not let him impose his lifestyle on our children, nor on me because God said to train up a child in the way he should go and when he is old, he will not depart from it. I believed in the Word of God then and I believe in the Word of God now; so there was no turning back to the life God had delivered me from. I stood firm in my faith, no matter what it cost me. I had a relationship with God and I was determined to keep it.

CHAPTER NINE

Coming To the End of Myself with God

After going through the family reunion and the ordeal with my ex, I began to question my life as a wife to him. I can remember my former Pastor saying to me in a meeting that no matter what anybody says concerning my marriage that I have gone far and beyond my call of duty as a wife to my husband. He knew that I was questioning myself and he said to me, "I want you to go home and pray with your husband and I want you to do the praying. He strongly voiced the fact that I should do the praying; He told me that I was to pray in the Spirit and God was going to give me the answer for my destiny. I did what I was instructed to do by my Pastor. I had always had a trusted relationship with my Spiritual Fathers in the gospel. It did not matter who My Spiritual

Fathers were because if God had placed them in my life to be the watchman of my soul then I respected them as such. One thing I had learned concerning the things of God was that whatever advice the man of God gave; it was my responsibility to obey it. I never doubted what they would say because I understood that if I was given false information from them then God was going to whole him responsible for misleading me. I placed my life in the hand of God through his servants.

I have always respected the role and position of the man of God and no one could cause me to go against them. I did not care what I heard about them or what I knew about them. I respected the fact that they belonged to God. In addition, that concept and knowledge have gotten me a long ways in my walk with God. God has opened doors for me that no man can close because of my faithfulness to His people.

I can remember one Sunday morning we were in Worship service and the Spirit of the Lord came in like a flood, as Acts the second chapter describes Him, and took complete control of the service to a point that when I embraced the Pastor's wife with a hug, we both were thrown apart from each other. She fell against the banister of the pulpit and I fell backward on the floor. The atmosphere was so powerful that it left an impression on the entire body. The next day, I was coming home from Jones and noticed that two of the church head deacons were visiting one of the church members. I kid you not, it was as if the Holy Spirit took my spirit into the mist of these men and I hear their conversation inside of this man's home.

The conversation was dealing with what had gone on at the church that Sunday. The Pastor and his wife was a major part of their conversation and so was I because I had announced the called to the ministry. That day plays repeatedly in my head even now because God had sent a word of warning to the body and I did not know what it all meant. The owner of the house was having a problem with what God was doing through the Holy Spirit and spoke against it. He voiced his opinion to other members, fought everything that was going on in the church. He was so heavy in my spirit all that day and that night on the Monday after that Sunday. I finally receive peace in my spirit about 2 O'clock A.M. that Tuesday morning. Therefore, I was able to sleep and not wonder about what it all meant.

After awakening the next morning, preparing to leave for school, the phone rings. One of the members of the church had called to inform me of what had happened to the man that spoke against what God was doing through the Holy Spirit. She asked me if I had heard that Mr. So-in-So died at 2 O'clock that morning.

I could not believe my ears. I was lost for words because that was the time that I had ceased to having him heavy in my spirit. I was shocked by her news. I knew that what this woman had shared with me had a lot to do with what I had felt in my spirit.

I finished getting dress for school and seeking God for understanding to what He was doing with me. I questioned myself to why this man was in my spirit and now he was dead. I went on to school trying hard to get passed this ordeal and pray for wisdom from God. After getting home from school, I searched for answers to this mystery. I asked God that if this is You dealing with me, then please show Yourself through your Word. If this is You, then when I see those other two men that was in the conversation with this man, let me see it in their faces when they see me coming.

On the day of this man's funeral, I was walking into the Church from the side door when I ran into one of the deacons who was at this man's house the day before he died and that man looked at me like he was scared to death to see me coming through the door. I spoke to the deacon and kept walking; and when I got around to the other side of the Church, I ran into the other deacon that was at this man's house the same day. I spoke to him as well and he did the same as the other man had done and that scared me even the more to know that God had allowed this to happen to let me and others know that He was real in my life and the lives of His people. One thing that I learned through that situation was that no matter what we think of others and their relationship with God, God knows who we are and what He has called us too. Who are we to question Him (God)? So much was happening with me that left me baffled, but I realized and I knew God was in control.

I also knew soon or later I was going to have to deal with running from my past and Doc was a major part of my past. I spent most of my life running from him, not wanting to face the fact that he had control over me and there were no way I could be complete in Christ without facing that fact in my life. Even when God brought that fiery trial back to my remembrance, I was still trying to fight it. God will put us in a place with Him that will cause us to shut up and listen.

In 1997, I moved to Hattiesburg with the intention of being on my own, with my children and the Lord. However, God had a different plan from what I had in mind. Through the Holy Spirit, God was building the life that He had planned for me all along. I was now walking in His Devine Will, which involved Doc. I was now in a place where I had to shut up and listen to what Doc had to say. We began to share things with each other that I had never known existed. I remember Doc telling me about the day he came by my parent's house to make it right with me because he had seen his Dad in a dream and his Dad told him that if he was not going to do right by me then he needed to leave me alone. He stated to him that I was not an ordinary young woman, and that there was something special about me that God had ordained. I could have died when he told me that because I knew that God had spoken to Doc through his Dad from the Spirit rim. There was a lot that he mentioned that no one knew but me. He talked about the house that God had shown me that I would own one day; he even showed me the blueprint; the car that I dreamed of owing, which he now drives. I am telling you that nobody knows anything about me when it comes to my relationship with God Almighty.

After getting settled in the new apartment, children settled in school, the next thing was to seek God on where to attend Sunday morning church services. I was still traveling to my home church for about six months, visited a few times at House of Prayer, but was waiting for an answer from God. Doc would invite me to attend services with him but I would always tell him no I could not because I was seeking an answer from God. I did not want my life to revolve around the fact that Doc was living in Hattiesburg too. I did not move because of him and I was not going to allow the enemy to cause me think that I was here because of him. I knew that God was the reason for my being in Hattiesburg. After waiting on an answer from God for six months, God then spoke to me to attend services with Doc. I call him up, asked him what time to be ready for service because I was going to attend his church that Sunday.

I remember asking God so many questions in my spirit that when I walked into the sanctuary of Mt. Olive Missionary Baptist Church I knew I was in the right place where God wanted me to be. God began to reveal everything that I could think to ask. After being in my apartment for a while, God began to open a door for me to move into a house in Rawls Springs which I needed to be anyway because my children was going to school with Doc's children but we were living in the Hattiesburg School District. My children would live with Doc through the week because I was still working at night at Ellisville State School and going to classes at Jones every morning until twelve noon.

In 1999, I was no longer working at Ellisville State School and was completing my last few hours of classes at Jones. I ended up going to summer school in order to pass college algebra, after which I could not pass at Jones so I transferred to USM. I passed the course and ended up changing my major to Psychology. Toward the end of taking my last few hours of Psychology, I began to struggle with those courses and I got to the point of wondering what in the world was happening to me. All of a sudden, I was having trouble in my studies. I ended up being placed on Academic probation for two semesters and the third semester being suspended. All while this was going on, I am seeking God to why this is happening.

God took my mind back to 1996, the original plan he had set for my life. I had to go back and finish the original course God had set for me. There were no shorts cuts for me because God was ordering my footsteps in His Word and I had to go through the way He had laid out for me. I was reminded of what my former pastor had spoken over the pulpit to me concerning the fact that God had His hands on me and nothing I did outside of the Will of God would prosper for me. I saw that prophecy being revealed right before my eyes.

So during the semester that I was suspended in the spring of 2003, I went back to Jones took a course that I did not need, Art Appreciation to be exact and finished my degree. I graduated from Jones in May of 2003 with an Associate of Art Degree in Childcare. My suspension was up at USM in the fall of 2004; so I enrolled again at USM to finish those thirteen hours I had left there. I graduated in May 2004 with a Bachelor's of Science Degree in Psychology. Therefore, my life again was back on track with God and I moved in His presence. It was at that time when God had restored order in my life that I began to sense the call to the office of a prophet even stronger.   The unction that I had being receiving earlier in my life was now back. However, this time I had a different attitude toward the things that was happening, as we will discuss in the next chapter. God had finally brought me to the place where He wanted me to be. My life in the Lord changed dramatically after that.

•CHAPTER TEN•

Call to the Office of a Prophetess by God

This is right where God wanted me to be all the time but I was afraid to go. I never said to God that I did not want to go, I simply said God I do not know how to go, I do not know what you want from me. Teach me how to be what you have called me to be. I had received an AA degree in Childcare in May 2003, I was licensed to preach the gospel in June 2003, and I graduated with a BS degree in Psychology in May 2004. God had set the table for me in the presence of my enemies; those who said that I will never be anything, those who wanted to see me fail in life, and all I had to do was walk in what God had done in my life. I was told that I would never make it as a woman preacher; I was told that God did not call me to preach and I myself was saying those same things to myself, but God proved Himself before the eyes of my critics including me.

Oh! God, how could I have doubted you when you have being the source of everything I had gone through? How you had brought me through so much heartache and pain? My faith escaladed in my belief in God after all that I had gone through. I was no longer afraid of what God was showing me and I was no longer bother by what people thought. If they could not deal with what God was doing in my life, I just did not do things in their presences because the Word of God tells us that if eating meat offend our brother then do not eat it in front of them, so I learned how to wait on God and move at His command. Times were getting harder and harder for me to bear and I kept hearing the voice of the Lord saying, "Cast all your burdens on me for I care for you". The more I lead on the Lord, more the pain and the hurt I was going through started to feel as though I can do this, I could go through this because my Master is with me. I was being criticized for what I believed in; I was told that I was from the devil, I was told that God do not have prophets anymore. I was told that Jesus was the last prophet that walked the earth and I said to that individual He lives in me. Therefore, if He (Jesus) is living in me and in you then there are still prophets present in the world today.

We must understand that things did not cease just because Jesus went to be with the Father. He is still our present help in our time of need. How can I say that He was when He still exists? Come on everybody do that make any sense at all. How can I deny the power there of?

Jesus said in John 16:7-11; "Nevertheless I tell you the truth; it is expedient for you that I go away; for if I go not away, the Comforter will not come unto you; but if I depart, I will send him to you. And when he is come, he will reprove the world of sin, and of righteousness, and of judgment; of sin, because they believe not on me; of righteousness, because I go to my Father, and ye see me no more; of judgment, because the prince of this world is judged. Jesus goes on to say in verse 12; "I have yet many things to say unto you, but ye cannot bear them now. Howbeit when he, the Spirit of truth, is come, he will guide you into all truth; for he shall not speak of himself; but whatsoever he shall hear, that shall he speak; and he will shew (show) you thing to come. He shall glorify me; for he shall receive of mine, and shall shew (show) it unto you. All things that the Father hath are mine: therefore said I that he shall take of mine, and shall shew (show) it unto you (KJV).

The Spirit of the Lord is present with us today to perform the things of our Lord and Savior Jesus the Christ. As I began to progress through the call that God had on my life, I learn boldness in the Holy Spirit and allowed him to teach me the things that Jesus had spoken of in John 16. I was very scared to step out and still am at time even today.

I can remember in May 2004, this young lady was on her way to Jones Jr. College to turn in a final exam paper when she was hit head on by a truck driving on the wrong side of the road. Once they got her out of the car, she was flown to the hospital in Jackson.

After the doctors had gotten her stabilized in ICU, I received a call from some of the members from my home church. This individual began to give me a report on what had happened and what the doctors were saying; the whole time she was talking, I was listening to the voice of the Lord. This child was on 100% life support and was not breathing on her own. I was called several other times after that and the last time I received a call from this person, there was a pressing in my spirit concerning the situation. I did not know weather God was saying for me to go to the hospital, or what He was telling me to do.

Therefore, I began to pray. "God I know that you are not finished with this child's life and I know that you have called her into the ministry; I know that You have not moved her into the place of ministry that you called her too. So clarify your voice to me. I prayed that prayer on a Thursday night at 9:00 p.m.

About two hours later, my friend called me and I did not give her time to say a word; I said to her we need to go to Jackson and her words to me were you sense that too. I say yes I do; so we made plans to go the next morning. Visiting hours at the hospital were fifteen minutes every hour. The whole time we were traveling to Jackson, the Spirit of the Lord kept whispering the word BRAIN. I told my friend what was happening. We made it to Jackson around 12:30 p.m. and the next visiting time was at 1:00. Therefore, I sat in meditation listening to what God was saying to me in hopes that He would make it plain to why He kept whispering the word BRAIN.

After arriving to the hospital, we finally found the waiting area and as I sat there while my friend was talking to another member from our home church, God tune my ears in on a part of their conversation. The young woman was telling my friend that since we had not seen the young woman who had being in the accident, she would go ahead and leave and let us visit in her place since she had being there at the beginning of the accident. Therefore, she left the area.

Well, we kept sitting there in the waiting room and I began

to notice that the whole time of our being there, not one member of the family was present and by that time the Holy Spirit led me to look at the clock. I looked up and it was 1:00 p.m., so I turned to my friend and said to her we need to find that ICU. I told her that we are going to stop the first white coat that passes us in the hallway. The minute we walked out into the hallway four or five white coats walked passed us and we stopped them and asked if they could tell us were the ICU was on that floor. They pointed to the right of us and the ICU was just around the corner.

When we got around to the ICU, the young woman that was sitting in the waiting area with us was standing in line waiting to go in to visit. She never bothered to come and get us; so I turned to my friend and said "God is going to do something in this place today because the enemy is at work".

My friend and I never talked about the mission the whole time we were there at the hospital; we just moved at God's command; we were on one accord to what God was doing. We never tried to get in to see the child. We just stood there waiting for the right moment to move. The sister who were handling the visiting time to ensure that all the family members had a chance to go in to see their sister came over to my friend and told her that she could go in, but my friend said to her no she, meaning me, needs to go in with me.

We walked into that room where the young woman was lying and the minute our foot touched the floor, it was as if the glory of God filled that room. I focused my eyes on the child's head and noticed that another one of the sisters was standing by her bedside stroking her brain; so I began to listening to the voice of God. I asked Him what now God? He began to give me instructions. He told me to lay hands on her arm and her legs. I did as I was told; He then told me to go around to the other side of the bed and lay hands on the sister who was stroking her brain. As I did what I was told to do, my friend laid her hands on me and we began to intercede for that child of God. I do not know what the others were saying, but all I said was in the name of Jesus.

By that time, the sister came back into the room and said it was time for us to leave, so we left. We were not out of the room a split second when that same sister who had asked us to leave the room came out and said the doctors said to keep praying, keep doing what you are doing because that young woman was now breathing 41% on her own. We began to praise God for what He was doing. We went back to the waiting area to pray with the family before we left and the devil was still on his job just as he was with the blind man and the healing Jesus did in the ninth chapter of St. John.

By the time I got back to Hattiesburg that evening, that child was now breathing 65% on her own and today she is alive and well. I will let nothing or no one shake my faith in God because I know what God can do and will do if we just trust Him to move when He tells us to move.

Devine order is what God is teaching his people. We must learn to walk in Devine order if we want things to change in our lives and in our families. We must seek to obey God no matter the cost. We must know that we know in whom we trust because the enemy do not care nothing about how anointed we may think we are, the devil is not thinking about how must Word we feel that we know because he knows the Word too. The one thing that gives us power over the devil is obedience to the Word and Will of our Father God from the son Jesus through the Holy Spirit.

I can remember that in May 2004 when I graduated from USM, our revival was going on at Mt. Olive Baptist Church. It was the last night of the revival and I was sitting at USM in my graduation cap and grown and was saying please hurry up, get finish with the ceremony so I can get to church because not only was I graduating from college, I was also graduating to a new dimension in my walk with the Lord. God was taking me to a new place in Him and I was excited about that.

The minister was just in the first point of his message when I walked into the church. He made a statement that prepared me for that new dimension. He said, "Some of you are going to the next level but know that "New levels brings new devils", and God knows that was the truth. I started being attacked within every area of my life in such a way that I found joy in knowing that I was being persecuted for righteousness sake. I found joy in knowing that God counted me worthy to go through what I was going through.

What God was doing for me was putting the finishing touches on my self-will attitude, doing away with anything that were not like Him, it had to go. I found myself many times lying out in the floor face down at home, crying out to God to help me. The pain that I was in was unbearable; talk about the refiner's fire, God had me right were He wanted me. I will be lying to you if I told you that it felt good because it did not, but I was glad when they said unto me, let us go into the house of the Lord. I was glad when He said no weapons form against me shall prosper, I was glad when He told me that He loved me and because He loved me, He chastens me. Glory to His Name because He is worthy to be praise, He is all that I have, please Lord do not take your presences from me.

Therefore, the crushing process is mainly the threshing floor where I can meet God in my trying times, in my good times, and my just want to be times. He is my source, He is my every thing, He is my lifeline, and I want so much to introduce you to Him. You may be reading this book right now and realize that you don't have a personal relationship with my Jesus. You see He is so good to me that I take personal ownership. But He can be that same thing to you as well; all you have to do is confess that you are a sinner, believe in your heart that He is the Son of God, that He died for your sins, and that He rose again the third day then ye shall be saved. That is all it takes. It is that simple. Why don't you give your life to Him today? He loves you more than you will ever know.

You have tried everything else now why not try

"Jesus"

He is truly your answer to life problems and situations.
He is truly the way, the life, and the truth. I dare you to try

Him

Today, this day in Jesus' name. Amen!

ABOUT THE AUTHOR

The Author of this book, Lora Johnson-Posey, has been moved by God to share her life story from the beginning to now. I trust that you have already prayed and asked God to minister to you as you read about this life of another person that can also be a life changing experience for you as well.

Lora has a heart after God's own heart and a heart for this nation. She is all about doing what God has called, commissioned, and commanded her to do. She is all about kingdom building and has a desire to see all God's people saved. Not only saved but also walking in all God has for us.

Sunday the 17th of February, our Pastor, Arthur L. Siggers, announced that Sister and brother Posey had gotten married. On that day, I begin to notice that she was a peculiar person. I was thinking this person was sanctified and holy and I was right she is both.

Around March or April 2003, we both announced our calling to preach God's Word. We started communicating and would talk sometimes to early the next morning. All credit goes to God for our coming together. What I learned was she is a prophet sent by God to build, encourage, direct and correct—"OUCHE". I think some of her famous words are, "WHAT DID GOD SAY ABOUT IT". I was blessed to have her book read to me over the phone and I know that it will bless you as well.

Lora A. Johnson-Posey graduated from Collins High School in May of 1978. She attending Jones Jr. College after graduating from high school, and majored in Childcare & Development, but dropped out in 1982. She returned to Jones Jr. College in August of 1996 and ended up transferred to the University of Southern Mississippi (USM) after she could not pass a College algebra course she needed to graduate from Jones. She passed the course at USM but changed her major to Psychology. She ran into some problems that stemmed from her dropping out of Jones in 1982, which lead to her being suspended from USM for academic progress.

While being suspended from USM, she returned to Jones and majored in Art Appreciations. She graduated from Jones in May of 2003 with an Associates of Arts Degree in Childcare. In June of 2003, she was licensed to preach the gospel under the leadership of Arthur L. Siggers and the Mt. Olive Church Family. She returned to USM in August of 2004, graduated from USM in May of 2004 with a Bachelors of Science Degree in Psychology.

In August of 2004, she attended Williams Carey College, majored in Religion, and was inducted into The National Dean's List of honoring America's outstanding College students around the world. Her accomplishment has being sent out to thousands of libraries, colleges, universities, and the Library of Congress. She later transferred to AmericanInterContinnual Online College in May of 2005 where she is majoring in the Master of Education program. She will graduate with her Master in Education on March 11, 2006.

Lora Posey is a prophet walking in the office of and is sent out to birth others into the kingdom. If you want to be blessed continue reading and may God bless you.

Karla J Mitchell

Sister in Christ

Made in the USA
Coppell, TX
23 April 2022

76950512R00073